Teaching Tips

105 Ways to Increase Motivation & Learning

Spence Rogers

and the Peak Learning Systems' Team

Peak Learning Systems, Inc.

Evergreen, Colorado

Teaching Tips: 105 Ways to Increase Motivation & Learning

published by

Peak Learning Systems
6784 S. Olympus Drive
Evergreen, CO 80439-5312
Telephone: (303) 679-9780

E-mail: peaklearn@aol.com
Website: http://www.peaklearn.com

Publisher's Cataloging-in-Publication
(Provided by Quality Books, Inc.)

Rogers, Spence.
   Teaching tips : 105 ways to increase motivation & learning / Spence Rogers and the Peak Learning Systems' Team. -- 1st ed.
   p. cm.
   Includes index.
   LCCN: 99-74442
   ISBN: 1-889852-13-9

   1. Teaching. 2. Motivation in education.
   3. Classroom management. I. Peak Learning Systems.
   II. Title.

LB1025.3.R64 1999   371.102
                    QBI99-904

Teaching Tips

105 Ways to Increase Motivation & Learning

Spence Rogers

and the Peak Learning Systems' Team

Notes

Acknowledgements

We would like to thank the following members of the Peak Learning Systems' Team for their contributions to this resource:

Spence Rogers
Shari Graham
Lisa Renard
Susan Tomaszewski
Roz Rogers
Michael Rogers

In addition, we would like to thank the countless educators and students who have contributed to our understanding and professional development over the years.

Notes

Table of Contents

Introduction to Teaching Tips: 105 Ways to Increase Motivation & Learning 1-8

    About Motivation 3

    How to Use This Book 5

    Two Key Principles 7

Chapter 1: Setting Up the Classroom 9-22

    Align the Visuals 11

    Arrange Seating for Flexibility, Movement, and Visibility 13

    Ensure Easy Visibility and Effective Visuals 15

    Keep it Ship Shape 17

    Maintain a Personal Inspiration Wall 19

    Provide Bright, Full-Spectrum Lighting 21

viii

Notes

Chapter 2: Building and Maintaining Relationships 23-62

Apologize for What Cannot Be Made Instructionally Right for Learning 25

Be Authentic: Require Quality from Students 27

Dignify, Dignify, Dignify 29

Draw Positive Energy to Get Over the Humps 31

Encourage Students to Mark Their Territory 33

Ensure Value to the Students 35

Explain "*The Why*" for Instructional Decisions 37

Exude Positive Energy 39

Focus on Leadership 41

Focus on the Color of Their Socks 43

Foster Safe, Caring Relationships 45

Greet Students as They Enter 47

Keep Students Emotionally Safe 49

Notes

Chapter 2: Building and Maintaining Relationships *(continued)*

Make Learning Easier without Lowering Standards 51

Manage Context – Not Students 53

Meet Students' Human Needs – Three Tips 55

Monitor and Adjust for Five Essential Feelings 57

Unlock Their Motivation to Learn 59

Use Inviting Language – Four Tips 61

Chapter 3: Quick Tips for Increasing Motivation and Learning 63-112

Ask "Why?" Differently 65

Avoid Red, Orange, and Yellow Ink 67

Balance Novelty and Ritual 69

Build Safety and Quality into Groups 71

Display Important Concepts on the Wall 73

Notes

Chapter 3: Quick Tips for Increasing Motivation & Learning *(continued)*

Display Main Points as They Are Learned – Two Tips 75

Engage Students within 90 Seconds 77

Establish Teaching Positions 79

Get Everything Ready Before the Students Enter 81

Have Students Stand Every 10 to 12 Minutes 83

Keep it Fast Paced 85

Limit Time - Don't Let Anyone Finish 87

Listen for the Lull When Using Cooperative Structures 89

Memory Boosters – Six Tips 91

Prepare and Use Value Added Activities 93

Provide Objectives, Topics, and Flow Up-Front 95

Separate Concepts with Colors 97

Start on Time 99

Notes

Chapter 3: Quick Tips for Increasing Motivation & Learning *(continued)*

Use Brain Writing Before Brain Storming 101

Use Color to Convey Importance 103

Use Music for Transitions 105

Use "Spoonful of Sugar" – Five Tips 107

Use the 10-2 Rule – Eight Useable Ideas in One 109

Use "We Are Here" Concept Maps 111

Chapter 4: Content Tips for Increasing Motivation & Learning 113-142

Concretize Learning – Four Quick Tips 115

Connect the Content to Positive, Emotionally Charged Experiences from Outside of School 117

Create a Purpose for Tasks 119

Elicit Physical Representations 121

Involve Students in Direction and Standard Setting 123

Notes

Chapter 4: Content Tips for Increasing Motivation and Learning *(continued)*

PQR – Praise, Question, Refine 125

Promote Thinking to Go Past Just Knowing 127

Provide for "Motivating" Feedback 129

Put Content to Music 131

"Remember and Try It Again" to Correct Procedures 133

Teach Procedures Up-Front 135

Use Partner Review 137

Use Self-Directed Student Licenses 139

Use Valued Audiences – Seven Tips 141

Chapter 5: Assessment, Evaluation, Testing, and Grading Tips 143-166

Check for Validity 145

Eliminate Extra Credit 147

Notes

Chapter 5: Assessment, Evaluation, Testing, & Grading Tips *(continued)*

Engage Students in Tracking Progress - Not Grades 149

Grade for Enhanced Motivation – Five Tips 151

Provide Options for Assessment and Evaluation 153

Raise Standards – Give Take-a-Chance or Quality Cards 155

Reduce Extrinsic Motivators 157

Separate Assessment from Evaluation 159

Use Coaching Rubrics – Preferably Student Developed 161

Used Delayed Testing and Distributed Practice 163

Use Recognition and Correction Cards 165

Index: Alphabetical Listing of Tips by Concept 167-175

Resources from Peak Learning Systems 177

Workshops from Peak Learning Systems 179

How to Reach Peak Learning Systems 181

Notes

Introduction to ...

Teaching Tips:
105 Ways to
Increase Motivation & Learning

Notes

About Motivation

Motivation is a term we use to label a human being's *focusing of energy that is caused by a desire or a need.* We believe that all people, including students, are

intrinsically motivated to learn – they just may not be motivated to learn what we have to teach. However, since there are many successful, highly fulfilled adults who are not motivated to learn what we teach, it doesn't surprise us that many students in our classes aren't motivated to learn it either. This doesn't mean that what we teach isn't important, it just means that we are faced with the complex problem of creating a classroom environment that unlocks our students intrinsic motivation to learn and channels that energy toward what we have to teach.

We often hear the question, *"How can I motivate my students?"* We would like to suggest that what we should be asking instead is, *"What is it that my students are highly motivated to have, and how can I use that in my teaching so my students will want to be there and to be successful?"* This collection of tips is designed to provide numerous options for doing just that. Another and more extensive resource for support in this area is the book ***Motivation & Learning*** (Peak Learning Systems).

Notes

How to Use this Book

No tip or strategy alone should make the difference. Instead, it's a whole collection of strategies, and tips, combined with the commitment to a set of principles that together build an environment and set of relationships that result in increased student motivation in our classrooms.

As you use these ideas, please focus most on *building relationships* with a strong foundation built on respect, trust, high expectations, challenging standards, and a commitment to the needs of people. This includes peoples' needs for enjoyment, belonging, autonomy, meaningful involvement, safety, purpose, and true success. The tips presented here are powerful tools to help in building these relationships.

We suggest selecting one tip at a time, focusing each day on improving with it until it feels internalized, and then selecting a new one to add to your repertoire. Another suggestion is to proceed through the tips at a rate of one per week until they are all comfortably in place for you and your students.

With each of the tips, the specifics of how to do it are not as important as the commitment to relationships felt by yourself and the students. As teachers, we have an obligation to adapt others' ideas to be consistent with the needs and realities within our own teaching setting. As long as we hold true to the principles behind the strategy, we will be successful.

Notes

Two Key Principles

for Unlocking Students Intrinsic Motivation to Learn

1. Manage Context – Not Students

People, not just students, tend to resent being managed by someone else; however, they do tend to enjoy working with excellent leaders. Excellent leaders focus on creating and managing context (environment, conditions, situations) in which people want to work hard, engage, make a difference, and in which they are willing to take risks. Poor leaders (people with whom others do not want to work or follow) tend to *try* to manage people by trying to get them to do things in preprescribed ways and timelines.

Effective teachers are excellent leaders.

2. Operate from Understanding

To be a successful leader requires adherence to Stephen Covey's assertion from *The Seven Habits of Highly Effective People* – "Seek first to understand ... " By doing this well, we are able to determine who our students truly are, what their needs are, how they think, and what is important to them – all of which are critical to our functioning effectively as leaders who know how to unlock our students' intrinsic motivation to learn.

Notes

Chapter 1. . .

Setting Up
the Classroom

Notes

Align the Visuals

Some students become uncomfortable and less receptive to learning when visuals appear haphazard, out of alignment, or imbalanced to them.

Take the time to make certain that the top of the overhead image is straight with the top of the screen and that the image is centered. Also, move the overhead projector and screen until the image is as large as possible while still clearly focused.

Align posters on the wall so that if they are all straight up and down or deliberately tilted, the top edges/points or the horizontal centerlines are all aligned or well balanced.

Notes

Arrange Seating for Flexibility, Movement, and Visibility: Four Tips

Arrange the desks or tables so that they can be moved easily to accommodate different activities. The following are several options to consider:

1. Seats can be clumped so that two to four students are sitting together for quick teamwork. *(Caution: Teams greater than two usually don't function effectively until they have been taught group process skills.)*

2. Arrange the seating in a large circle for whole class discussions.

3. Use a chevron pattern when all attention is to be focused in one place.

4. When using a chevron or rows and columns, slightly bunch the seats so that there are aisles all around and a "plus" shaped pair of aisles though the horizontal and vertical centers.

Front

Notes

Ensure Easy Visibility and Effective Visuals

When students have difficulty seeing anything that is important to their learning, they tend to become put off and lose motivation for two reasons:

1. When visuals are not prepared well enough for them to be easily seen, many students interpret it as indicating that the teacher doesn't care enough about them, the content, or their learning.
2. Because humans have the need to feel smart, capable, competent, and successful, students tend to lose interest in anything that they believe is too difficult.

Put yourself in the role of the student with the poorest eyesight in your classroom. For every visual you use, check all the positions in the classroom to be certain it can be *easily* seen and read.

*A **rule of thumb*** for creating visuals, such as transparencies and slides, is to print the visual on 8.5 x 11 inch paper, set it on the floor, stand on a sturdy enough chair or table, and make sure you can easily read it. If in doubt, ask the students.

For posters, transparencies, and slides use high contrast colors. A blue background with white letters is great for computer graphics. A white background with black, blue, purple or green ink is good – they're easy to see! Avoid red except for titles, underlining, circling, or high-lighting.

Notes

Keep It "Ship Shape"

For many of our students, it is very important that the classroom be neat, clean, and well organized. When it is not, some students will become uncomfortable enough that it interferes with their learning. Take time to be certain that …

- there aren't piles of materials out, or if there must be, they are very neat and placed out of the way
- the teacher's desk, tables, and other work surfaces are clutter free and neatly organized
- chalk trays and other areas are dust free
- all spills are cleaned before students enter class
- repairs are made and graffiti has been removed
- any trash on the floor or elsewhere has been properly thrown away before the students enter.

An added bonus to keeping the classroom "ship shape" is that many students, parents, and administrators perceive it to mean that we care about what we do, about our students, and about our roles as professionals.

Notes

Maintain a Personal Inspiration Wall

Set aside a section of a wall for inspiration. This is best done on the back wall because it is not as effective as the others for instruction.

A personal inspiration wall is a place where each student has something displayed that is personally important. There are several options for this.

- On the first day of class, have the students write an inspirational message that is important to them, draw a picture that conveys the message, sign it, and hang it on the inspiration wall.
- Have each student create a personal poster/ representation, share it with the class, and hang it on the inspiration wall.

- See *Motivation & Learning* for other ideas including a memory wall or a wall of student selected pictures.

Inspiration walls are essential to building a sense of community because they establish the sharing and staking of territory. These walls are so important to the students that they must be well maintained.

Notes

Provide Bright, Full-Spectrum Lighting

Classrooms are places where people come together to work hard and learn well. Human beings are not nocturnal animals – we are well developed to function during the day.

Ensure that the lighting in the classroom is bright and as close to natural as possible. Open the blinds to flood the room with natural lighting but protect students from having to work in direct sunlight. If the windows are inadequate for flooding the room with bright, indirect, natural lighting, try augmenting with incandescent, or full spectrum lights.

Limit the use of the florescent lights in classrooms to adding brightness to the natural lighting. When the florescent light is too bright it can raise anxiety. If forced to choose between a heavy dose of florescent lighting or dim lighting, do some experiments and involve the students in ensuring optimal conditions.

21

Notes

Chapter 2. . .

Building and Maintaining Relationships

Notes

Apologize for What Can NOT be Made Right for Learning

When students know that we sincerely care about them and their needs, they are far more likely to tolerate a poor situation and continue to maintain high levels of motivation and learning in our classrooms. Therefore, it is important to know, sense, or discover when something is not right, and fix it. If it can't be fixed immediately, then students need to know when it will be. If it can't be fixed at all, then it helps if we apologize for the condition and ask the students to please bear with us. The fact that we care enough to have acknowledged the problem will help gain forgiveness and support from most students.

Some things to apologize for and fix immediately, or at least to explain as to why they are as they are include:

- temperature
- small print on visuals
- wrong color print
- seating conditions
- legibility of materials
- time limitations
- light limitations
- restroom conditions

Notes

Be Authentic: Require Quality from Students

Imagine A+ Quality from Everyone

Employers demand quality. Spouses demand quality. Consumers demand quality. Why shouldn't there be some tasks in classrooms for which all students are expected to refine their efforts until they have earned an "A" for quality? Imagine the benefits of teaching students that with some tasks, people are not done until they've done the task well.

Demanding that every task be turned in "on a due date" when it will be graded is based on the old, assembly line approach when timeliness was stressed more than quality. With much of what is expected in life today, quality reigns as more important than timeliness. In an attempt to match the demands students will face in the "real world," shift some tasks from a demand for timeliness to a demand for quality. Also, try shifting some tests from being tools to evaluate learning and assign grades to tools for checking the extent of learning for further coaching until quality is achieved and good grades are earned.

Notes

Dignify, Dignify, Dignify

There are no bad answers – just bad questions. Sometimes our questions really aren't worded or framed well enough. Other times, students may be responding from different and/or unexpected perspectives. If we ask a question before students have enough background to answer correctly, then we have run the risk of diminished motivation that can result from feelings of not appearing successful before others. Ask questions to prompt thinking, not to catch students as right or wrong.

Students' motivation to contribute begins to fade rapidly as soon as they believe that their dignity is suffering. Above all else, protect each student's dignity from his/her perspective.

Strive to find and point out what's right in any response. If this can't be done, probe to find out what prompted a student's thinking and dignify the student by validating it. If the student's perspective is different from what you have been promoting or looking for, simply point out that a lot of people share that perspective and ask the students, "How many of us know someone with a similar perspective?" Then continue to build from where the class left off before being diverted.

Relationships

Notes

Draw Positive Energy to Get Over the Humps

At any time in our classrooms, there is a chance that at least one student is not totally enthralled with the content, the instructional activity, or both.

The students must know that if an instructional activity is not consistent with their favorite approach, at least they won't feel embarrassed during it. They must also believe that the activity will not last too long.

Because both positive and negative attitudes can be very contagious, and because negative attitudes can bring a whole group down, use cheers and positive prompts to surface the positive attitudes.

- "If you feel good about ___, please yell, "YES!""
- "What are the best or most important points about _____?"

Be a cheerleader for students and the content, and foster the students becoming cheerleaders too!

Notes

Encourage Students to Mark Their Territory

It is important for people to share in the ownership of living and workspaces. People who have moved in together usually encourage one another to display personal items such as photographs and pictures. Most people find ways to decorate/mark their workspace with things such as family photos, degrees, certificates, plants, music systems, or inspirational posters. Students benefit from the same opportunity.

On the first day of meeting as a class, encourage the students to draw something important, write an expression that is inspiring to them, or bring in a photograph to display. Set aside wall space and label it with a poster that may say something like, "Who We Are." Ask the students to display what they have created on this special wall.

Caution: Do not grade or mark what they put here. Ask only that it carry the permission of their parents and yourself to ensure the protection of family, school, and community values.

Notes

Ensure Value to the Students

People tend to be motivated enough to work at learning anything if they value it or the learning experience enough. There are four ways this can happen:

1. What the students are being asked to learn *solves a problem they believe they have and they believe is important to solve.* This is one reason why teaching students from families that support education is relatively easy. It is also why teaching Drivers' Training is easier than teaching many other subjects.

2. The students are being asked to learn about something that is *personally interesting* to them. This is why connecting what we are teaching to topics such as dinosaurs, animals, cars, and street issues can help to increase motivation *for those students who are interested in these things.*

3. The instructional activities are ones that the students consider *fun*.

4. The classroom is a place the students would like to be because it's at least better than everywhere else, in their opinion.

Caution: The popular rush for authenticity and relevance is not enough for motivation, though it does help for some students. Building authenticity ensures that students will be taught how what they are learning is used outside of school, but many students still may not care. Relevance is a personal issue. What one student considers relevant, another may not. Something is relevant *to someone* if they perceive and value an application, connection, or interest. In other words, the word *relevant* prompts the question, "Relevant to whom?"

Notes

Explain "The Why" for Instructional Decisions

Students tend to support and cooperate with what we are doing instructionally when they understand why we believe it is a good thing to do or why we have to do it. We can do this by having them tell us what they have found is effective instructionally, or explain to them why it makes learning easier and more effective for them when we use a particular instructional strategy.

One strategy for doing this with students is to tell them that we want to use ideas they have about what works best. Then ask them to recall when they have had "really powerful effective learning experiences." Give them some examples and definition (during scouts, during sports, or during a great project in which they learned a lot). Ask them what characteristics of the experience made it so powerful. Their answers will give permission for all kinds of active involvement, communication of ideas, and application of content.

If they don't have the experiences to provide the rich responses yet, then just explain how something like, "We know from research that people tend to remember longer with less work those concepts that they explain to someone else. Therefore, what we will be doing today is taking turns explaining to one another…"

Notes

Exude Positive Energy

Enthusiasm is contagious – don't try to teach without it! Do what it takes to be full of energy and excitement for your students– as a person and for your content.

We have all seen good coaches, either in movies or in our own lives, use the power of intense enthusiasm. It works on the field, on the court, on the stage, and in the classroom. People tend to feel better and work harder when they are around others who are excited and enthusiastic – but it must be real. Use pep talks, excited words, peppy music, and cheers. If it's important to pump up athletes, actors, debaters, and work teams, then isn't it important to do so for learners?

Never stop searching for new ways to show your excitement and enthusiasm. Stay on the look out for enthusiastic people, and borrow things they do that convey their enthusiasm.

If you think this is a good idea, please yell, "YES!"

Notes

Focus on Leadership

A leader is someone with whom others will go where they wouldn't normally go by themselves.

We have many students who have decided they will never have any use for a lot of what we are teaching and have little to no interest in investing a lot of energy into learning what we have to offer.

The key is leadership.

As a means to hone our leadership skills and increase the chance that our students will want to exceed expectations, we can study books such as *Enlightened Leadership* by Doug Krug and Ed Oakley and *Principle Centered Leadership* by Stephen Covey. These and others like them are loaded with powerful techniques for creating environments in which people will go far beyond where they would go without an effective leader.

One leadership tip comes to us from a saying attributed to Mao Zedong (Mao Tse-tung, 1893-1976), *"A sign of a great leader is everybody else thinks it's their idea."* Design leadership activities in the classroom that include engaging students in discovery and involvement in the development of criteria, rules, rubrics, assessment options, and learning activities.

Notes

Focus on the Color of Their Socks

Many people can sense when others don't like them or agree with them on an issue that is very important to them. When a student senses dislike or disagreement from us, there is a strong chance the student's motivation to perform in our classroom will drop rapidly.

There is a trick that can help. If we sense we are about to feel a disliking for someone or what they are saying, find something about the student we like and focus on it. If the only thing that appears likeable at the moment is the color of his or her socks, then *focus on the color of his or her socks!*

Notes

Foster Safe, Caring Relationships

Students tend to work harder and take more learning risks with people with whom they feel a strong and positive relationship. Because there are so many students in a classroom environment, it is essential that good relationships are established throughout the classroom. Foster the following relationships for high levels of motivation:

- between each and every student
- between each student and yourself
- between each student and the content

Use class and team building activities regularly.

Involve students in determining, monitoring, and adhering to the class rules and acceptable behaviors. Help students find benefits for being successful in learning what you have to teach.

Notes

Greet Students as They Enter

Let students know they are welcome in the classroom and that you care about them.

Stand at the door, in the hallway, or just inside the classroom to greet your students as they enter. If this is not possible, make eye contact with each student and in some way acknowledge him/her before beginning instruction.

Notes

Keep Students Emotionally Safe

Students tend to work harder and take more learning risks when they feel emotionally safe in the classroom. By *emotionally safe* we mean that the students do not fear that they will be embarrassed. Embarrassment can come from exposure of anything *the students* consider embarrassing – which might include personal information they want kept secret or anything they consider to be a significant lack of knowledge or skills.

Part of the difficulty with keeping the classroom emotionally safe is that each student has his or her own threshold for emotional safety. Using common sense to protect students is essential, but not enough. It is also important to periodically survey the students in a "safe" way to determine what we need to avoid or to do differently.

As a starting point, eliminate all sarcasm. Also eliminate the threat of the use of public displays of student work that shows a lack of knowledge, skills, or creativity from the students' perspective.

Notes

Make Learning Easier without Lowering Standards

Because human beings are often motivated by feelings of success, and also because they tend to become demotivated when not feeling successful, it is essential to seek and use strategies that will make the learning easier without lowering the standards.

When teachers lower standards for students, it typically will not solve the problem of students needing to feel success for sustained motivation. It's hard to feel successful when we know that high standards are not upheld for us.

Strategies like energizers, carousel graffiti, partner review, mastery learning, think-pair-share, and many others tend to make learning easier and thus increase the likelihood the students will feel successful without lowering standards.

Notes

Manage Context – Not Students

People tend to resent being managed, however, they tend to enjoy being led by a good leader. Good leaders focus on creating and managing the context (environment and situations) in which people want to work hard, engage, and make a difference. Poor leaders (people with whom others do not want to work or follow) tend to try to manage others by telling them what to do, when to do it, how to do it, and what to think.

If a leader is someone who others will follow to where they wouldn't normally go by themselves, then it makes sense to do what good leaders do – "Manage Context, Not People." As shared by Doug Krug and Ed Oakley in their book ***Enlightened Leadership*** (1993, Simon & Schuster). To be successful at doing this requires following Stephen Covey's observation from ***The Seven Habits of Highly Effective People*** – "Seek first to understand." By doing this, we are able to determine the needs of our students so we can build an environment in which they maintain their intrinsic motivation to learn and succeed.

Notes

Meet Students' Human Needs – Three Tips

1. **Feed the Brain.** Learning is hard work, and working hard requires adequate food and water. Provide healthy, energy boosting, nutritional supplements in the classroom if you can, or as a minimum, allow them between classes. Be careful to avoid the problems that can be associated with high sugar foods. Many fruits, cheeses,  crackers, popcorn, vegetables, breads, and milk can all help. Experiment with your students to find the right combinations for your learners, yourself, the time of day, and the classroom conditions.

2. **Water the Body.** Be certain your students have access to water whenever they feel thirsty. If leaving the classroom regularly is a problem, try providing a jug of water and drinking cups.

3. **Provide Relief.** When learners feel a need to use a restroom, attention to learning drops. Find a way to make it safe for learners to be able to use the restroom whenever the need arises.

Providing food, water, and restroom visits won't motivate anyone, but withholding them can lead to significant damage to relationships, motivation, and learning.

Notes

Monitor and Adjust for Five Essential Feelings

To maintain high levels of motivation in our classroom, our students need to feel each of the following:

- Safe (physically and emotionally)
- Autonomous (free and independent)
- Successful (competent, creative, skilled, knowledgeable)
- Valued and cared for (a sense of love and belonging)
- Enjoyment

It is important to monitor these feelings for each of our students, and if a student is not feeling these, then it is time to modify or change our instructional strategies until the feelings are present.   A common misperception with this idea is that we need to lower standards – not

true! If a student perceives that we have lowered standards, he will be able to logically conclude that he is not truly being successful and we have lost what we are trying to achieve.

In ***Motivation & Learning*** (Peak Learning Systems), a survey is included that can be modified and used with various student groups and age levels.

Relationships

Notes

Unlock Their Motivation to Learn

Focus on unlocking students' intrinsic motivation to learn. Maybe we can't motivate anyone else to learn; but we can build an environment to elicit students intrinsic motivation. Abandon all language that refers to motivating students – it blinds us from understanding what truly needs to be done.

Motivation to learn is intrinsic. A preponderance of studies suggests that the use of extrinsic motivators to increase motivation in a classroom actually reduces motivation to learn as well as the quality of performance over time. An extrinsic motivator is anything we might use or do that meets the following three criteria:

- It has either positive or negative value to the students
- The students know about it in advance
- We are using it in an attempt to change students' attitudes or behavior.

We have an improved chance to unlock our students' intrinsic motivation to learn if we:

1. Make learning easier without lowering standards
2. Foster safe, respecting, trusting relationships throughout the classroom
3. Design instruction so students learn how to apply or use what is being taught
4. Ensure that students consistently gain evidence of success, mastery, and progress toward mastery
5. Meaningfully involve students in direction, methods, decisions, and criteria.

Notes

Use Inviting Language – Four Tips

In an effort to build a community of learners in which we all work together for a common cause, it is important that our language conveys a sense of community and not one of building barriers.

1. Express the objectives using "we will" instead of "the students will."

2. Say things like, "Today we will be …" rather than, "I would like you to …"

3. Survey by saying something like, "How many of us …?" as opposed to "How many of you …?"

4. Avoid "you" language in conveying ideas that inadvertently tells others what they are or have been thinking or doing. Rather than, "It's difficult for you to find your way in the mall." Try something like, "It can be difficult for people to find their way in the mall." or "It's difficult for me to find my way in the mall."

Notes

62

Chapter 3...

Quick Tips for Increasing Motivation & Learning

Notes

Ask "Why?" Differently

When students are asked "*Why*?" outside of school, often it is a situation in which someone believes the student has done something wrong. For example, *"Why did you put peanut butter in the VCR?"* After a while, many students react defensively as soon as they hear the word "*why*" at the beginning of a sentence. Find other ways of asking "Why?" by considering prompts such as the following:

- What might be the reasons behind …?
- Will you please explain your reasoning …?
- Will you please tell me more about …?
- How come?
- What might be the reasons for …?

Notes

Avoid Red, Orange, and Yellow Ink

Not only do they tend to raise anxiety, but red, orange, and yellow are colors that are hard for people to read. Use them to circle, highlight, or underline, but NEVER to write.

If we wish a word or phrase to jump off the board or transparency, then we can use red. However, it is important to check to be certain what is in red can be easily read from the entire room by any student. Sometimes it is necessary to actually write the word a little bigger so that it can be read as easily as the other words.

Notes

Balance Novelty and Ritual

Students need a mixture of novelty and ritual if we wish to maintain high levels of motivation and learning in our classroom.

Novelty is used to bring students to peak attention, make learning fun, and create a positive emotional response to enhance learning and memory. Too much novelty becomes exhausting if it isn't broken up by ritual. Students need time to slow down and rest.

Ritual is important because it creates a safe environment and a time when we can mentally relax – both of which are critical for learning and motivation. The problem is that an environment that is all ritual (known and predictable) becomes very boring and learning diminishes. Use classroom procedures and content for establishing ritual – always post concepts on the wall and always ask the students to enter or leave the classroom in the same way. Vary instructional approaches and strategies each day to build excitement and fun.

Notes

Build Safety and Quality into Groups - Three Tips

To help maintain their intrinsic motivation to learn and produce quality work, use the following quick tips during cooperative structures or group activities:

1. Until class and team building activities have established adequate feelings of safety on the part of each student, give the students full or partial choice regarding group mates.

2. Before student perceptions of safety are established, it is also important to allow the students to choose their group roles (recorder, facilitator, reporter).

3. Deliberately plan on only three to five groups reporting out from a group activity at a time. If choice as to order for reporting is provided, then some groups can take advantage of the extra time to refine their work.

Notes

Display Important Concepts on the Wall

Make it easier for students to learn concepts by "seeding" (preparing) their minds in advance and providing visuals throughout the room by displaying concepts on the wall.

Create and display posters that represent, express, or visually convey the major concepts that you will be teaching. Use short phrases, powerful words, symbols, or bulleted lists. Hang the posters high on the front and side walls of the classroom – reserve the back wall for announcements, assignments, inspirational posters, and student work.

One possible adaptation is to ask students to develop the posters and display them. Another suggestion is to ask the students to prepare the posters at the end of a unit and then use them later (with permission) when you begin the unit with a new group of students.

Notes

Display Main Points as They Are Learned or Presented – 2 Tips

As students are learning concepts, make certain that you, a student, or a group of students create large visual displays of the concepts. This helps the students learn by creating a visual representation to reinforce what they are hearing, seeing, or doing.

This strategy can be done on large chart or butcher paper in one or both of the following ways:

1. Building a *numbered* list of the main points as they become apparent.
2. Developing a concept map, preferably with icons, connecting the main ideas as they unfold.
3. Constructing a timeline as events are addressed.

Be certain that the displays are large enough and displayed high enough for all students to see. Also, avoid red ink except to highlight.

If they don't have the experiences to provide the rich responses yet, then just explain how something like, "We know from research that people tend to remember longer with less work, those concepts that they explain to someone else. Therefore, what we will be doing today is taking turns explaining to one another…"

Notes

Engage Students within 90 Seconds

When starting class, it's important that every student is actively engaged almost immediately. This can be done through humor, questions for the group, or an activity.

This does several things simultaneously:

1. It conveys that the classroom is a community of learners
2. It uses time well for learning or relationship building, both of which are important to increased motivation and learning
3. It boosts energy.

Specific ideas include:

- Start class with jokes or fun stories
- Have something meaningful on the students' desks, tables, or work areas for them to begin working on as soon as they enter the classroom
- Ask questions as they enter the classroom that require engagement by every student
- Refer to *Motivation & Learning* (Peak Learning Systems) for dozens of additional ideas.

Notes

Establish Teaching Positions

Establish different positions in the classroom that you will always use for specific purposes.

The students will learn to associate our position with what is to be happening at any given time. This will help trigger the students' attention when needed and facilitate learning by making it easier to visually separate the different types of information or activities in the classroom.

Most importantly – establish one position from which you gain the students' attention, and always go to that position to get their attention. Other positions you may wish to establish include ones for:

- Getting attention
- Making announcements
- Giving assignments
- Presenting information
- Giving directions
- Telling inspirational stories
- Asking questions
- Presenting discipline

Notes

Get Everything Ready Before the Students Enter

Before the students enter the classroom, prepare everything you will need for the lesson and make certain it is all in the right places for speed and minimal confusion.

As adults, we prefer it when stores, doctors, restaurants, and teachers have taken the time and made the effort to prepare completely before our arrival. The same tends to be true for our students. Not only does this save valuable instructional time, it helps to ensure that learning is not unnecessarily interrupted. We also send the message that we care by taking the time to prepare in advance.

An added bonus is that when everything is well prepared, we can move very rapidly with NO lulls. Lulls can lead to boredom, mischief, and diminished energy and motivation.

Notes

Have Students Stand Every 10 to 12 Minutes

Increase alertness, blood flow, oxygen flow, energy, motivation and learning by asking the students to stand up about once every 10 to 12 minutes. Before asking them to stand, it is also helpful to ask them to take a deep breath.

Once they are standing, engage them in one of the many *10–2 Rule* (Refer to *Use the 10–2 Rule* in this book) processing activities while standing or have them move around.

Caution: Protect students who find standing painful or difficult. Encourage any students with physical

difficulties involving standing to move their shoulders and arms about once every 10 to 12 minutes.

Notes

Keep It Fast Paced

People like things to keep moving unless they are just plain exhausted and need a rest. In addition, there are students who will find ways to fill down time, no matter how short it is.

Students' ways of filling this time may not always be a good use of time. For high energy, highly motivated people, down time imposed on them can lead to frustration, anger, boredom, and/or apathy. Plan everything in advance so that once class begins, every-

thing can be kept moving at a fast pace. Be certain to have "value added activities" planned and other meaningful or fun fillers that keep the pace up if a lull begins to develop. If nothing else, while keeping everything moving quickly, you will be exuding energy which will impact the students positively.

Notes

Limit Time – Don't Let Anyone Finish

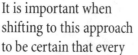

When students are engaged in instructional activities in which they are asked to brainstorm or to develop concepts, they finish at different rates. This variation typically leads to management problems in classrooms, which can then lead to students feeling frustration, boredom, anger, or incompetence, which can result in diminished motivation and learning.

When involving students in these types of brainstorming or concept building discussion activities, rather than allowing enough time for each student or group to finish, limit the time just enough so that no single person or group can finish. Then, use other small group or whole group processing strategies to reach the intended outcome. This way there is no down time for students who finish early and no feelings of stupidity by those who don't finish.

It is important when shifting to this approach to be certain that every student understands why you are doing it and expect not to finish as individuals. Be certain they understand that you are going to help them save time by building on the collective thinking within the classroom. Explain or draw from them that since different people approach thinking in different ways, a whole group can generate a whole perspective when the contributions of the individuals are combined.

Notes

Listen for the Lull When Using Cooperative Structures

It is not always necessary or desirable to announce to the students a set time period for a discussion in which you are about to ask them to engage. Time limits tend to be arbitrary and may be either too long or too short. Neither one is a good situation.

Typically, when we ask students to discuss a question or issue with others, we can expect a pattern in the noise level within the classroom. It will gradually increase as more and more of them engage, then it will maintain a relatively high level as the students are highly engaged, and finally the noise level will begin to drop as some groups draw close to completion. As soon as you hear the drop beginning, bring the whole group back together for whole group sharing.

Caution: If the issue being discussed is deep and complex, go past the first lull which indicates the students are just beginning to really wrestle with the topic. Wait for the second or third lull.

Instead of a time limit, try saying something like, "Let's see how many points each team can develop before I call 'time.'"

Notes

Memory Boosters - Six Tips

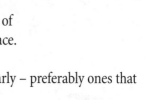

1. When asking the students to memorize a list, have them form pairs and say the list over and over again to each other until you say stop.

2. Clump the things you want people to remember so that there are never more than seven, and preferably three, five, or fewer clumps with each clump having five or fewer points.

3. Involve as many senses as possible by creating ways that multiple senses become involved.

4. Have the students move from place to place in the classroom as you present different concepts for them to learn about. Periodically have them recall where they were standing when the concept was first introduced.

5. With each new unit, develop a new seating arrangement so that each student or group of students has a new place.

6. Plan fun breaks regularly – preferably ones that involve laughter.

Notes

Prepare and Use Value Added Activities

Many times in teaching, things happen that prevent us from starting at the time we expect to start.

Sometimes students are unavoidably detained, or something in our planning has a glitch, and we just can't start on time. Another similar problem occurs when students are pulled from class early. In either case, it is important to have and use *value added activities*.

A value added activity is one that extends, enriches, expands, or reinforces the learning and that can be used suddenly with students to add value, but when other students cannot be involved, they will not miss essential content.

An example is to use an activity like Partner Review (see page 137) or any similar ideas presented here or in *Motivation & Learning* (Peak Learning Systems).

Notes

Provide Objectives, Topics, and Flow Up-Front

Many students don't care and aren't affected by whether or not they know where they are going or how they will progress. There are others who become frustrated and confused without this information.

At the beginning of each day, lesson, unit, and year, let the students know the objectives (in student level language and actions), the topics, and the planned sequence of events. Do it quickly and simply and everyone will benefit.

Notes

Separate Concepts with Colors

When students are learning about different concepts, try using different colors for the different concepts. This will make it much easier for visual preference learners while it also makes it easier for others as well.

Once a pattern of colors is selected for the concepts, be certain to stick with that pattern – deviation will confuse many students.

While using this tip, try to avoid the use of red unless it is to underline or circle.

Use colors that are easy to read by all students at a distance. Try blue, black, purple, green, and brown.

If you are "using blue" to signify important information, then clarify this temporary shift with the students in advance.

Notes

Start on Time

Always start on time in order to establish a desirable pattern, honor those who make it there on time, and to meet the needs of many who are highly task oriented.

Be certain to be completely prepared in advance so it is possible to "hit the ground running" and start precisely on time. If this becomes impossible, or if students are unavoidably detained from getting to class on time, announce to the students why you will be starting late and engage them in a value added activity while you prepare to start officially.

Notes

Use Brain Writing Before Brainstorming

Some call this *think time*, which it is, but on a slightly grander scale.

Before students share their thinking in small or whole groups, it is important to ensure adequate time for individual thinking. This can be done by having them write or draw their thoughts in response to a prompt before sharing in groups.

Brain Writing provides an opportunity for shy students to formulate their thinking before sharing with others. It also gives more time to students who need it to formulate their thoughts, think more deeply, or who may be wrestling with a question which is new to them.

Notes

Use Color to Convey Importance

Tell the students up-front what color you will use while presenting information for that which is important to learn for the "test" or other "graded" events. Try blue for what they are expected to learn. Assure them that you will use other colors like black, green, or purple for other items like announcements, assignments, and directions for activities. Why? Because we are making it easier for visual preference learners to quickly separate out what is important to know.

Be careful to be consistent! Ask the students to help you help them and point out immediately if you ever accidentally use a "wrong" color. This will not only help everyone learn, it will focus the students on essential learning.

Notes

Use Music for Transitions

Use music for transitions, breaks, before starting, and as the students are leaving the classroom. Select music that will have the desired effect for the students and situations. Baroque can have a calming effect and many believe it can increase the brain's ability to learn. Others prefer to use up-beat music to create an energizing, positive atmosphere to help foster positive mindsets.

Students will want to be involved in the selection of the music. When students are allowed to bring in classroom-appropriate music, they often feel affirmed and valued as unique and worthwhile individuals. Be certain the music they select meets the following criteria:

- It's effective for its intended mood effect for the students.

- If it has lyrics, they are appropriate for the community and the classroom.

CD players with remotes tend to be easiest for making rapid shifts in music.

Notes

Use a "Spoonful of Sugar" Five Tips for Helping "the Content Go Down"

Plan lessons so that each student will believe he is getting a "spoonful of sugar." For students who love our content, we don't need to plan anything extra. For the others, it is important to find something that they are already motivated to learn about, do, or experience and find ways to incorporate these things into the lesson. Ways to help achieve this include:

1. Conducting thematic units around topics or concepts that are of interest to the students

2. Utilize strategies that students find fun like Carousel Graffiti, Off the Wall Metaphors, and Partner Review

3. Encourage students to demonstrate their learning (based on your specific curriculum and standards) in alternative and fun ways of their choosing or design

4. Provide a few minutes each day for humorous, fun, or interesting stories

5. Put, or ask the students to put the content to song, metaphor, story, poem, or rap.

Notes

Use the 10 – 2 Rule – Eight Useable Ideas in One

The 10 – 2 Rule: No matter how the students are receiving knowledge or skills, interrupt the input about once every 10 minutes to allow for about 2 minutes for the students to process the learning.

We can allow for this by asking students to do any of the following:

1. Draw what they are learning
2. Sing or rap about it or represent it through dance
3. Explain it to someone else
4. Create a flow chart, simile, or metaphor
5. Explain how it is similar to something they already know

6. Explain how it makes sense
7. List the main points
8. Or any other active engagement of the students' minds in the processing of the facts, topics, concepts, procedures, or skills.

This strategy can be enhanced by ensuring that the students have to move or at least stand to complete whatever the processing task is. It is also helpful for processing activities that do not involve collaboration to have the students share with one another what they have done.

Notes

Use "We Are Here" Concept Maps

Most malls, airports, and other large and complex public areas have "You Are Here" maps displayed prominently to help people learn where they are and how to get where they are going. We can do the same thing with our classes.

Construct a large concept map of your curriculum.

Each time the class has addressed a concept, ask the students to indicate where they are on the map.

Each time you are about to begin a new concept, help the students to see where it is on the concept map and how it connects to what they have already learned.

Notes

Chapter 4...

Content Tips for Increasing Motivation & Learning

Notes

Concretize Learning – Four Tips

Start each lesson with instructional activities that engage every student in reviewing and/or extending the content of the previous lessons.

When students first enter the classroom, they are full of energy and in a prime state for mentally processing content. Take advantage of this to reinforce the learning from the previous day. Except in extreme circumstances, students don't truly learn anything on first exposure. Repetition from different perspectives and in different ways over time is important to learning.

Use any of the following four ways to help students concretize their learning from the previous lesson:

1. Develop and share concept maps of previous content
2. Develop and share flow charts of procedures or processes
3. Construct and share similes, metaphors, or connections
4. Take turns sharing points or connections.

Refer to **Motivation & Learning** (Peak Learning Systems) for even more ideas including "Walk About."

Notes

Connect the Content to Positive, Emotionally Charged Experiences from Outside of School

Students tend to remember content longest, understand it best, and value it the most, when it is connected to something they feel good about and understand already. Some strategies for doing this include:

1. Ask the students to develop "off-the-wall metaphors and similes" and to support them with deep and complete arguments. Example: Give three correct and meaningful ways that (a concept) could be said is like cotton candy.

2. Compare, or better yet, have the students compare the situations/reasons/concepts or procedures we're teaching to something positive that they feel good about from outside of school.

Notes

Create a Purpose for Tasks

People tend not to write letters, write reports, conduct research, create tables, or build models without having an intended purpose or use for their efforts. And yet, we often ask students to do these things without attaching a purpose, either real or fictitious, to make the task more authentic and/or possibly relevant to the students.

When developing an assignment like any of those listed above, attach a purpose. Possible ideas for this might include statements like:

"Your (note, poster, talk ...) is to be used to ...

- Persuade
- Teach
- Inform
- Excite
- Build awareness
- Present
- Support
- Defend
- Advise
- Prescribe

... (name an audience) and then identify a reason someone would want to do this.

Example: "We're going to write notes to friends who have been absent explaining what we learned this week and how to use it. Build in some questions for your friend to answer so you can check for his/her level of understanding."

Notes

Elicit Physical Representations

After teaching several concepts, ask the students to form groups of four to five people for a fun activity. Then ask each group to develop a physical way to represent each of the different concepts they have been learning. Give them some examples that may be used. Let them know that each group will be expected to work in unison to present to the class their physical representations and will be asked to explain how each of their representations could be construed to contain or exhibit the critical attributes of the concept it represents.

For example, if a concept being taught is "safety," the students may act like umpires in a baseball game as they indicate a runner is "safe."

Notes

Involve Students in Direction and Standard Setting

People tend to hit the targets they set for themselves. When students are involved in the development of the standards and directions (not the curriculum or academic standards) for the classroom and tasks, they take ownership while developing a deeper understanding of the expectations. In other words, the process of developing procedures, direction, standards, and options is often more important than what is actually developed.

Have the students analyze sets of exemplary and lesser quality examples of whatever they are to be ultimately developing or doing in order to determine the critical attributes of the exemplars. Through processes like these which engage students in the development of "shared guidelines and expectations" based on exter-nally established standards, we create an environment in which students develop deep understanding and commitment. (See page 78 of *Motivation & Learning* – Peak Learning Systems.)

Students can be involved easily and successfully in developing exemplary:

- Coaching rubrics
- Scoring rubrics
- Classroom rules
- Homework criteria
- Effective options for demonstrating knowledge, understanding, or skills and abilities
- Specific criteria for an assignment or task.

Notes

PQR – Praise, Question, Refine

When students are asked to share their efforts and provide constructive input to one another, they often don't know a good way to do this. The following is an adaptation of a process that we learned from Jay McTighe.

1. Ask each student or group of students to present to another student/group what they have done in a factual, straightforward manner. Just the facts! As this is happening, the listener(s) can ask clarification questions only and the answers are to be strictly clarifying – no editorializing anywhere.

2. Have the sharing student/group move away and work on something else while the listening student/group generates a T-chart. The T-chart is to have on one side a list of specific good points about what was shared. The other side is to have a list of questions to help the sharing student/group see possible "loop-holes" or glitches to be fixed. The questions are to be non-judgmental.

3. The listening student/group now goes off to work on something else while the sharer(s) decide what refinements (if any) should be made based on the questions.

Notes

Promote Thinking to Go Past Just Knowing

Develop a repertoire of questions and strategies for promoting thinking. Many students will tend to function on only a surface level by expecting us to provide whatever they are to learn. Expect students to formulate, not just give responses. Expect them to build, combine, synthesize, and extend.

Ask questions like:

- What do you think?
- What are reasonable solutions?
- How does that connect with what we already know?
- If we were to pursue that thinking, where might it take us?
- What could be the implications?
- How is what you are saying similar to what happened before?
- How is that different?
- What would be a convincing defense for that position?
- What might be reasonable, alternate approaches?
- How could we have used this before?
- What could be the benefits?
- What might be the liabilities?

Notes

Provide for "Motivating" Feedback

in Addition to Giving Teacher Input

Feedback, not input, is very important to sustained motivation. What most people refer to as feedback is actually "input from the teacher." Input is what we as teachers (or students) provide to a student to convey strengths, weaknesses, and recommendations. Feedback is helpful information obtained by students to provide guidance and recognition for their thinking or efforts. Feedback that is essential for sustained motivation meets all of the following five criteria:

1. It is learner-controlled. The student is in control of when and to what extent the feedback will be.
2. The feedback is corrective or evidence of successful progress or mastery.
3. It is timely – not necessarily immediate. Sometimes feedback that is corrective is not appreciated or desired immediately – only the learner knows when it is best.
4. The feedback is regular – feedback opportunities should be provided during instruction or learning activities at least once every 10-20 minutes.
5. It's non-judgmental. Effective feedback provides specific information as to what is correct and what is not – without praise or criticism.

Motivating feedback is more what people receive as they are driving in traffic or what happens as they share their thinking or progress in groups.

Notes

Put Content to Music

When asked to say the alphabet to ourselves, many of us still hear the ABC song we learned in elementary school. For centuries, people have used songs, chants, rhythm, and poetry to boost memory, so why not continue in our classrooms?

Create and teach a song, rap, or chant that contains important content, or better yet, ask the kids to do it. In either case, memory will be enhanced.

Notes

"Remember and Try It Again" to Correct Procedures

Particularly at the beginning of a school term, students will test our commitment to building a positive learning community. Some students will test all year long. They may be looking for signals from us that our positive, community-building words are not matched by our actions.

When students test us by breaking the rules the class has established or by ignoring procedures in the classroom, one way to respectfully demonstrate our commitment to a safe learning community is to offer a chance to "Remember and Try It Again."

As soon as a student or group of students breaks a rule or forgets to follow a procedure, ask the students to stop, guide them in remembering the rule/procedure and then ask them to do it correctly. Never attack the student, just

"Remember and Try It Again."

For example, if a student grabs a pencil from her neighbor's desk without asking, we can say, "It seems we may have forgotten our procedures for borrowing someone else's supplies, let's pause for a moment to recall our procedures and practice them until we are doing them correctly again."

Be careful not to blame, punish, or reward – just focus on being a supportive coach helping the students to recall, correct, and practice. Remember to thank them for doing it well.

Notes

Teach Procedures Up-Front

Establish a well structured, efficiently run classroom environment by identifying and teaching procedures up-front. Procedures that will make the classroom a more pleasant and effective place for all may include:

- Turning in work
- Classroom entrance and dismissal
- Getting student attention after a group discussion or activity
- Sharpening pencils
- Restroom use

When teaching procedures, always teach them separately from teaching content. This will help to ensure that the students take us seriously, focus on the procedure, and learn it well. The following are important steps for teaching procedures:

1. Explain, or draw from the students, why the procedure is important
2. Explain and model the procedure
3. Check verbally for understanding
4. Have the students do the procedure with nurturing, non-judgmental coaching until it is done correctly
5. Have the students then immediately practice the procedure at least one time – "practice makes permanent"
6. Before the students first need to use the procedure, remind and check for understanding
7. Correct incorrect procedures immediately in a non-judgmental, nurturing way.

Notes

Teaching Tips © 2005 Peak Learning Systems (303) 679-9780

Use "Partner Review"

When students have enough knowledge about the content that you have been teaching to recall and expand on it for at least five minutes, try partner review as a fun way to engage the students.

1. Ask the students to form groups of two. If there is an odd number of students, ask someone to serve as an observer.
2. Ask the students in each pair to decide who will play the role of "Red River" and who will play the role of "Mesa Verde" – two arbitrarily selected nicknames.
3. Ask the students to stick to the following rules as they review together for a full five minutes:
   - They may use any notes and resources as they share for the full time.
   - Only the person you stipulate (Red River or Mesa Verde) is to be saying whatever he/she can remember from the material at a time.
   - The students are to switch who is talking immediately, back and forth, on your command. (Switch them every 20-40 seconds or whenever you see a student getting stuck.)
   - They are to try to avoid repeating themselves or one another.
   - They are **not** to ask questions of one another during the activity.
   - They are **not** to answer questions asked by their partner – they are only to say all that they can remember from the material or all the connections they can make.

Content Tips

Notes

Use Self-Directed Student Licenses

Students and homework don't always mix. Here is an idea that helps reduce the workload for us with homework and helps to improve attitudes and motivation in the classroom.

The Background: A state issues a driver's license to those citizens who desire the right to drive and are willing to prove they have met the criteria for doing so. Because of the manner a driver's license is handled by the state, it is not an extrinsic motivator, it is a natural consequence.

A Way to Improve Attitudes and Behavior with Homework: Discuss with your class the what's, why's, and how's of a driver's license. Make certain they understand that possession of a license is a choice made by a citizen and the state doesn't put any worth or value on it. They need to understand that a license is a "right" chosen and earned by a citizen, it can be lost for demonstration of lack of skills or judgment, and it is simply a natural consequence – not a bribe, threat, reward, or punishment.

Announce the existence of a "Self-Directed Student" license. It is not something every student will want, but it is an option for those who choose to make the decision to earn one and demonstrate the criteria to the teacher. It is the student's responsibility to arrange for the demonstration of the criteria which would probably include a history of good grades, following rules, and treating others with respect.

As long as students are in possession of a license, they may show it to receive full credit for any homework assignment that is considered practice of a skill or a knowledge building exercise. The license does not exempt students from tests, quizzes, assessments, projects, or evaluations, and the license can be lost just like a driver's license can be.

Notes

Use Valued Audiences for Increased Motivation – Seven Tips

Just as athletic and drama coaches have known for years, students tend to be more motivated to work hard and perform with quality when there is an audience they value or respect. There are many ways and audiences for us to use.

1. When using the 10 – 2 rule, have the students share with others what they have produced.
2. Display student work on the walls, ceiling, in published books/magazines, or in the hall.
3. Invite parents, members of the community, or other classes to watch as students present what they have learned or accomplished.
4. Ask the students to share with the person next to them what they just learned, heard, or understood.
5. Request that the students have their parents or another adult write them a note sharing why they like a piece of work, are proud of it, or how it shows excellence.
6. Have the students create web sites to display and receive feedback for their work.
7. Ask the students to form groups and use the Praise-Question-Refine strategy.

For a list of hundreds of more ideas for creating audiences, please refer to the book *The High Performance Toolbox* (Peak Learning Systems).

Notes

Chapter 5. . .

Assessment, Evaluation, Testing and Grading Tips

Notes

Check for Validity

When what we teach aligns with how we assess and evaluate student progress, the students do better. The result is increased motivation and learning in our classrooms.

Check all assessment and evaluation instruments for validity (alignment) with the following two questions:

1. Is it possible for a student to have the targeted learning and NOT be able to do this task well?

2. Is it possible for a student do to this task well and NOT truly have the targeted learning?

It's easy to fool ourselves with these two questions. Check your opinion with the opinion of colleagues and others both inside and outside your teaching assignment. If the answer to either question is "yes," modify the task until the answers to both questions are "no."

Notes

Eliminate Extra Credit

Extra credit is an extrinsic motivator that carries with it even more baggage than virtually all other extrinsic motivators.

Not only does it shift the focus from learning to earning credit, it also allows students to not learn and/or do well with something that we have already deemed to be important in our curriculum.

Let them redo, refine, enhance, enrich, and extend something they did not do well until they have done it excellently. Then they will have earned a better grade with something they were already asked to do. This holds students accountable for learning from the curriculum well and not being let "off the hook" for learning or doing something that is truly important.

Notes

Engage Students in Tracking Progress – NOT Grades

People tend to lose motivation when they believe they are not as successful as *they feel a need to be*. For many students, grades can be highly demotivating. Therefore, it is important to develop ways for students to track their progress in acquisition of skills, knowledge, concepts, ability or their progress toward mastery.

Asking students to track their grades, though certainly a worthwhile task, is NOT tracking progress. In fact, it is the demotivating effect of the grades on many students that makes this strategy so important. The following are ways we can ask the students to track their progress:

- Keep a list of topics studied, concepts understood, or skills developed.

- Create and use a graph or icon (like The United Way's thermometer) to monitor growth in knowledge.

- Keep a growth portfolio including regularly updated letters to the reader identifying specific evidence of progress in knowledge, skills, or abilities.

Notes

Grade for Enhanced Motivation – Five Tips

1. When grading, marking, or providing input on student work, use blue, black, green, or purple ink – never red or a reddish tone including orange or brown.

2. When possible, mark what the students have done correctly rather than what they have done incorrectly.

3. If a student is not satisfied with a grade or a mark, encourage them to improve their work and resubmit it for a higher one.

4. Involve students in the development of the criteria that will be used for determining grades through the analysis of exemplary work. (See *Standards of*

Excellence on Page 78 of ***Motivation & Learning*** (Peak Learning Systems).

5. Determine the three to five "things" th___ students re___ do well to b___ year." With___ require that___ refine until t___ an excellent g___

Notes

152

Provide Options for Assessment and Evaluation

Students enjoy options, but more importantly, they tend to resent not being involved in decisions that impact them.

Develop several ways students can show how much they have learned or how they are to learn what you are teaching. Encourage them to develop their own options for how to prove that they have learned.

When providing or encouraging options, be clear as to the specific criteria to be met, and ensure that the criteria are met.

Build a model

Compose a song

Write an essay

Write a poem

Notes

Raise Standards – Give *"Take-a-Chance"* or *"Quality"* Cards

Some tasks in life must be completed by a deadline with no chance or expectation for improvement and with no tolerance for finishing late. Job interviews fall in this category.

Other tasks in life require a quality performance, and though timeliness is important, lateness may be accepted because the quality of the performance is more important than its timeliness. The teaching of lessons is an example – if the students don't learn well enough one day, we typically reteach using different strategies the next day.

Try giving the students either *"Take-a Chance"* or *"Quality"* **Cards** to be used with the tasks for which the quality of performance is more important than timeliness. If the students have not met the *Quality Standards* for an excellent performance and grade by the imposed deadline, they turn in their cards which provides them with an agreed upon extension (not an exemption) to meet the standards.

Testing and Grading Tips

Notes

Reduce Extrinsic Motivators

Extrinsic motivators are defined to be anything that meets all of the following three criteria:

1. They have either positive or negative value to the students. Whatever they are, the students either want them (candy, points, extra credit) or don't want to have them (demerits, points removed, grounding, removal of recess).
2. They are known in advance by the students. "If you _____, then _____."
3. They are being used to change or modify behavior or attitude.

Extrinsic motivators tend to work in the short run while they tend to lower performance over time. They cause immediate desired boosts, but then they can lead to dependence, a need for more each time, and possibly resentment because they are an overt attempt to change behaviors or attitudes. Extrinsic motivators are not always bad – they can serve an immediate and important purpose. If there is a behavior that we absolutely need, and if we can't find any other way to get it, try an extrinsic motivator.

Cautions:

1. Reduce dependency slowly by changing the class environment and the instructional strategies so that extrinsic motivators can be gradually dropped.
2. There are differences between goals, natural consequences (positive and negative) and extrinsic motivators – be careful to understand the power of each.

Notes

Separate Assessment from Evaluation

"We can't fatten cows by weighing them." By the same token, we can't improve student learning by evaluating them and assigning grades. For motivation, it is important that we "feed" the students through teaching and assessing until they have reached a quality level. Then we can "weigh" them with evaluation and grades.

To **assess** is to gather information using specific criteria in order to determine what changes we need to make to improve performance. To **evaluate** is to gather information in order to generate a judgment, score, or grade. Assessment (being coached) is a motivating experience for many students, where as evaluation (being graded) tends to be demotivating for many.

At the classroom level, when we assess, the grades earned are changeable. (If the students are not allowed to improve their work to earn a better grade, we have evaluated – we didn't assess.) At the classroom level, when we evaluate, we generate grades and scores that are recorded in the book and are not subject to improvement by the students.

Tip: Assess until you know the students have mastered, then evaluate to produce the documentation for the grade book and transcripts. (See Mastery Learning in *Motivation & Learning* – Peak Learning Systems.)

Notes

Use Coaching Rubrics – Preferably Student Developed

In any given class, there are some tasks, probably at least three to five, that are vitally important to the students' continued learning. These tasks deserve coaching rubrics.

Coaching rubrics are lists of exemplary criteria for tasks that the students are expected to do excellently, and then they receive an excellent grade for what they have done. When coaching rubrics are used, the only thing that might lower a student's grade from an excellent one is if the student turns in their work significantly later than the recommended final deadline. With coaching rubrics, the students aren't done until all the criteria are met well, at least as well as shown by the exemplars that were used to develop the coaching rubric. The students are held accountable for the high quality of their work, and the amount of time it takes is allowed to vary. (With a scoring rubric, the students are done when the deadline occurs – the students are held accountable for timeliness and the quality of their work is allowed to vary.)

Coaching Rubrics are common place outside of school. Several examples include:

- The criteria for a driver's license – we get the license when all the criteria are met well enough and then our license is granted. We either meet the criteria and get a license, or we keep trying until we do. We aren't given graded licenses.
- The criteria for completing our grade book or for a child cleaning his/her room.
- The criteria for a report that a supervisor needs from an employee.

Coaching rubrics create a context with increased motivation, and scoring rubrics tend to create a context with variable (almost bell curve-like) motivation. (Please refer to page 78 of *Motivation & Learning* and Chapter 7 of *The High Performance Toolbox*.)

Notes

Use Delayed Testing and Distributed Practice

"Now I get it; I sure wish I could take the test now." How many times have we heard students say something like this a week or more after a test? Why do we test before the weekend or a vacation rather than after? How many times have we seen some students successfully cram for tests only to forget everything in a few days? When we test too early, we limit success and long-term retention.

The students who are getting the good grades are the ones who either fundamentally already know it or the ones who value grades enough to cram for good ones. The other students, the ones who tend to need the most support, are the ones who tend to earn lower grades – which only adds to the vicious circle toward failure, diminished motivation, and discipline problems. And, of course, there are many good grades going to students who really haven't learned anything yet.

Instead of testing at the end of a unit, conduct culminating activity to tie the unit together and then begin the next unit without the usual test. Each day devote some portion of class time and a portion of each homework assignment to reviewing and enriching activities with the previous unit's material (**Distributed Practice**). Whenever possible, help the students connect the material from the previous unit to the current one. Continue this for about three weeks and then administer the **Delayed Test**.

In addition, incorporate Mastery Learning for enhanced motivation & learning. (Refer to **Chapter 4 of *Motivation & Learning***, Peak Learning Systems, for additional support with Mastery Learning and Distributed Practice.)

Testing and Grading Tips

Notes

Use Recognition and Correction Cards

Almost all students enjoy being recognized for what they have done well. Similarly, almost all students need input for correction from time to time. The way they are delivered can be very effective for some students and highly demotivating for others.

Early on, ask the students to complete **Recognition & Correction** cards. The following steps work well for most classes with some obvious modifications based on maturity and trust levels:

1. Use group process to engage students in discovering differences in students' needs for recognition and corrective input.
2. Ask the students to complete **Recognition & Correction** cards.

3. On the front side of the cards with the students' names, have them tell you how they would like to be recognized for doing well. Give them some examples like "calling home," "pointing it out in front of the class," or just "a discreet nod."
4. Ask the students to tell you on the back of their cards how to provide corrective feedback when it is necessary to do so. Again, give them some examples.

As soon as you get the cards, start doing what they say!

Testing and Grading Tips

Notes

Index

Notes

Index

A – C

Asking Questions	29
Assessment	153, 159
Assessment and evaluation critical differences	159
Assessment and evaluation	153
Attitudes	31, 41
Authenticity	35
Brain writing	101
Building Relationships	5, 45, 47, 49, 77
Color	67, 97, 103
Color and Grading	151
Color of their socks	41
Color to convey importance	103
Colors to separate concepts	97
Concepts	73, 97
Concept Maps	111, 115
Concepts on the wall	73
Concretizing learning	115
Context – not students	53
Coaching rubrics	161
Create a purpose	119

D – F

Delayed testing and distributed practice	163
Dignify, dignify, dignify	29
Displaying main points	75
Distributed practice and delayed testing	163
Emotional experiences	117
Energy	31, 39
Energy, exude positive	39
Energy, draw positive to get over the humps	31
Engagement within 90 seconds	77
Evaluate	159
Evaluation & assessment	153, 159
Evaluation & assessment, critical differences	159

169

Notes

Extra credit   147

Extrinsic motivators   157

Feedback   129

Feedback, motivating   129

Feelings   57

Feelings, essential   57

G – L

Grades and marks for enhanced motivation   151

Greeting students   47

Groups   13, 71, 137, 165

Homework   123, 139

Human needs   55

Input, teacher   129

Inspiration wall   19

Inviting language   65

Involvement in directions and standard setting   123

Language   61, 65

Leadership   43, 53

Lighting   21

Lighting, full-spectrum, bright   21

Listening   89

Listen for the lull   81, 89

Lull   81, 85, 89

M – Q

Manage context   7, 53

Memory boosters   91, 131, 133

Motivation   25, 29, 51, 55, 57, 59, 69, 71, 81, 129, 139, 149, 151, 161, 163

Motivation key: make learning easier without lowering standards   51

Music   105

Music for transitions   105

Music, put content to   131

Novelty   69

Novelty and ritual   69

Objectives   61, 95

Objectives, topics, and flow up-front   95

Options   153

Organization   17

Notes

Pace, fast	85
Partner review	137
Personal inspiration	19, 33
Positioning	79
Praise, question, refine	125
Procedures, teaching up-front	135
Progress tracking	149
Promote thinking	127
Purpose for tasks	119
Quality	27, 71
Quality cards	155

R – T

Ready before the students enter	81
Recognition & correction cards	165
Red, orange, and yellow ink	67
Relationships	5, 45
Ritual	69
Ritual & novelty	69
Rubrics	123, 161
Rules	133, 137, 139
Safe (Safety)	49, 71

Safety, emotional	49, 71
Seating	13
Seating	13, 25
Self-directed student licenses	139
Ship shape	17
Spoonful of sugar	107
Standards	51
Standing every 10-12 minutes	83
Starting time	99
Take-a-chance cards	155
Teaching positions	79
Temperature	25
Ten–two rule	109
Territory marking	33
The why for instructional decisions	37
Timeliness	25, 27, 87, 89, 99, 129, 155
Time limits	87, 89

U – Z

Understanding	7
Validity	145
Value	33, 35

Notes

Value added activities   93
Value to the students   35
Valued audiences   141
Visibility   15
Visuals   11, 15, 73, 75, 79
We are here concept maps   111
What cannot be made instructionally right   25
Why   37, 65

Notes

Resources From Peak Learning Systems

The High Performance Toolbox: Succeeding with Performance Tasks, Projects, and Assessments by Spence Rogers and Shari Graham. Practical, teacher-tested guidelines, templates, strategies, tips and supporting examples for successfully using performance tasks and assessments as a part of a comprehensive approach to student learning and achievement.

Motivation & Learning: A Teacher's Guide to Building Excitement for Learning and Igniting the Drive for Quality by Spence Rogers and Shari Graham. Over 600 immediately usable ideas, strategies and tips with a supporting theoretical foundation to improve the quality of motivation, achievement, and student work.

Teaching Tips: 105 Ways to Increase Motivation & Learning by Spence Rogers and the Peak Learning Systems' Team. A collection of 105 easy-to-use, research supported and brain-compatible strategies and tips. Its foundation is a commitment to a set of principles that build an environment and relationships that unlock students' intrinsic motivation to learn and produce quality work. This resource is a great companion to *Motivation & Learning*.

Teaching Treasures: 229 Prompts to Make Learning by All a Dream Come True by Spence Rogers and the Peak Team. A collection of 229 easy-to-use, research supported and brain-compatible tips for teachers.

Teaching and Training Techniques: Lighting the Way to Performance Excellence: by Spence Rogers and Becky Graf. Essential tools for effective instruction.

21 Building Blocks Critical to Leaving No Child Behind: A Commitment to Excellence by Spence Rogers and the Peak Team. Critical components of effective classrooms and schools.

177

Index

Notes

Workshops from Peak Learning Systems

Workshops and Consulting. Workshops, consulting, and train-the-trainer sessions by the authors and their colleagues can be scheduled at your site. Each workshop will be custom-tailored to meet your specific needs and conducted in a manner consistent with best practices and research.

A sample listing of workshops, presentations, and keynote sessions

Increasing Student Motivation & Learning
Rubrics and Grading
Scoring and Coaching Rubrics
Strategies for Block Schedules
Classroom Assessments
Reaching Standards in Mathematics
Teaching Strategies for Differentiated Classrooms
Assessment Strategies for Differentiated Classrooms
Teaching and Training Techniques
Questioning Strategies that Promote Learning

Notes

How to Reach Peak Learning Systems

To order additional copies of this book, schedule presentations or workshops, or request information about any other resources from Peak Learning Systems, please call, fax, write, or e-mail us.

Telephone:	303-679-9780
Fax:	303-679-9781
Website:	http://www.peaklearn.com
E-mail:	Peaklearn@aol.com
Write:	6784 S. Olympus Dr.
	Evergreen, CO 80439-5312

Notes

Our thanks and gratitude to all the dedicated educators who tirelessly work with kids to make learning by all a dream come true.

We have enjoyed working on this book and we hope you will enjoy using it in your classrooms! We love hearing your ideas for increasing motivation and learning in the classroom. Please call us or e-mail us with any suggestions or ideas you think will help us improve this resource. Thank you!

Spence Rogers & The Peak Learning Systems' Team

**Peaklearn@aol.com
(303) 679-9780**